ELECTORAL REFORMS IN INDIA

SHEIKH MUZAMIL MOHD.

ISBN: 1511443111

ISBN-13: 978-1511443111

DEDICATION

This book is dedicated to my parents, teachers and friends.

CONTENTS

ACKNOWLEDGMENTS

All praises to almighty Allah for bestowing me self-confidence and courage, which made this dissertation a successful one.

I am very thankful to my guide and convener, **Dr. Narendra Ojha** for his valuable guidance, timely suggestions, and supervision. His dedication to the course of research has always been a source of encouragement to me. Special thanks go to head of social science dept. D.A.V.V. Indore (India) **Dr. kanahiya Ahuja**

And hearty gratitude is expressed to **Dr. Ashwini Kumar Sharma** and **Dr. Sanjay Jain** for providing all help and support to undertake this study.

I am also thankful to all dept. staff especially to **Sanjay Sir, Ajay Bhaiya, & Dada.**

I owe much to the library staff of central library of Devi Ahilya Vishwavidyalaya, Indore (MP), central library of Ujjain University and other institutes for providing me valuable material.

I am highly thankful to my family members especially my parents **Ghulam Mohammad Sheikh & Taja Beigum.**

I am also indebted to my friends and co-researchers, and others who provided me whole hearted support to complete this dissertation.

And finally I want to thank to the inspirational lines by ramz-e-yusuf

Zindaa ho to labb ki girra'h khol kar dekho,

Aisey khamosh na baitho, kuch bol kar dekho,

SHEIKH MUZAMIL MOHD.

1 ELECTORAL PROCESS IN INDIA

(A) Introduction

Viewed from any angle, whether political, social or psychological the electoral process in India is always being fascinating story, no matter whether it's national or state level. There is no other single event in India which offers such a great excitement, interests and thrill. Elections have contributed a lot to national cohesion and growth of democratic temper. Socially elections have been the great equalizer identical opportunities for exercising choice to entire electorate. All participate equally whether poor or rich, rural or urban, educated or illiterate, skilled or unskilled, male or female. Talking administratively, these have posed formidable challenges in the sheer organization and logistics which no other democracy in the world has to contend with.[1]

More importantly elections have became a way of life and an exercise of faith or Indian masses, successive elections have both enhanced and deepened the peoples commitment to the democracy. They have also made Indian voter fully conscious of the value of vote, and the power of ballot as the most impotent instrument of change. Every election is a potential turning point in the history of India, as elections shape the destiny of nation.[2]

Free and fare elections are integral part to democracy. It is through elections a free modern state is created or at least hopes to create amongst its citizens a sense of involvement in public affairs. Again, it is through popular elections that an elected government is clothed with authority and legitimacy. Elections symbolize the renewal of the consent of people, the only basis on which rests the claim of the rulers to govern in modern times. Furthermore imparts continuity in governance for it ensures peaceful, orderly replacement of the government and makes possible a smooth transfer of authority to new set of new leaders.[3]

---

[1] R, Meenu. <u>Elections 1998-A continuity in Coalition.</u> New Delhi: National Publishing, 1998. p.18

[2] Fadia, B.L. <u>Indian Government and Politics</u>. Agra: Sahitiya Bhawan, 2013. p.708

[3] Bhagat Anjana, kaw. <u>Elections and Electoral Reforms in India.</u> New Delhi: vikass publishing house pvt.ltd., 1996. p.2

Elections in India are considered to be the very backbone of the Indian democracy. Being a Parliamentary Republic, the citizens of India are trusted with the responsibility to choose the head of the country as well as of the state. There are both General and State elections that are held in the country based on the Federal structure of the Indian Republic.

India therefore adopted the Anglo-American majority system. The statute drawn up to govern Indian elections derived not only its content but even its name from British counterpart-the Representation of people Act. The system has been described as the fist-past -the-post system. The country is, as rule, divided into single member constituencies which elect their representatives not by an absolute majority but by a relative majority. The majority system is adopted in the hope that it will produce strong governments and a stable party system.[4]

The elections in India often transcend from being a mere political activity to a high publicized and often sensationalized national event, with clear cultural ramifications. The entire nation seems to suddenly come to life at the onset of the elections, particularly the General Elections. Even the assembly elections, which determine the state government, are events of great significance. All state elections are closely observed throughout the nation. Often the results of the state elections are considered to be clear indications of the mood of the nation. It is beyond doubt that free and fare elections are the cornerstones of democratic polity. It is also perhaps the most effective and undoubtedly the ultimate method of controlling and regulating the conduct of political elites. It's true that once the mandate for political governance is given, the ruling elites have more or less free hand, subject, of-course, to the constraints of the Constitution and operates laws, to carry on the business of governance as they please.[5]

(B) Significance / Importance

Elections in India provide the occasion for the widest degree of popular participation; they constitute the most important single arena for genuine competition between political groups; they are principal agency through which recruitment to a significant part of the political elites is affected; and they skill the resource which they especially call fourth figure prominently in political life in general. Elections in India are now seen not merely a useful indicators but actually as the event through

---

[4] ibid. p.12

[5] Op.cit. P.6

which the party system and hence, in a measure, the political system achieve their evolution[6]

Elections are generally thought of as integral feature of political system, as they are usually linked with political parties and other none-ascriptive organizations and processes in India, they are both 'modern' and 'modernizing' agencies, but also serve as links between 'modern' and 'traditional' sectors of Indian life and they are profoundly influenced by, as well as exert a profound influence upon, the nature of Indian political culture. The Indian experience has proved that they can function in essentially 'traditional' social system with an overwhelmingly illiterate population, and still serve the modern political goals of integration, nation building and development. In the process the social order becomes more closely identified with the political system and the political system develops a broader social base.[7]

Joseph Schumpeter describes elections as the heart of democracy. If representative democracy is only what is really practicable, there are elections which can make democracy feasible. It is very difficult to imagine the democracy without elections. Elections provide candidate from whom the voters choose their representatives; they make the government as well as the opposition: those who are able to have majority make the government and those who are not able to form the majority make opposition.[8]

The electoral system provides the mechanism which makes election possible. It specifies the officers/positions which are to b elected, the voters who are entitled to vote, the method as to how they would be vote, the constituencies from where the officials would be elected, the way the elections would be held. The electoral system, in fact includes both the election and electioneering. The elections make the representation possible.[9]

The foundation of democratic government lies in a high degree of participation of citizens in public affairs, civic matters and policy formulations in varied forms. The success of democracy largely

---

[6] WH Morris Jones .B, Gupta. India's Political Areas. Asian Survey: Interim Report On An Ecological Investigation June, 1969. p.399

[7] Fadia, B.L. Indian Government And Politics. Agra: Sahitiya Bhawan, 2013. p.707

[8] Arora, N.D. Political Science. New Delhi: Tata Megraw Hill Education Private Ltd., 2012. P.7.9

[9] Ibid. pp7.9-7.10

depends upon the faith of the people in the political system as well as political institutions. The faith and interest of general citizen population may be construed as vital elements for the growth and stability of democratic institutions. Therefore, legitimacy of institutions has to be judged by the general verdict of the people.

The study of general elections is quite necessary and even significant because, it attempts to unveil the extent of legitimacy of the ruling party as well as effectiveness of it. Besides, such a study serves the basic purpose of not only continuance of the legitimacy of the old legitimate but also an instrument of change and re-distribution of political power[10]

The mechanism of elections is viewed as a peaceful ballot revolution through which the omissions and commissions of the ruling authority are accounted, and on the other hand, the role and sincerity of the opposition parties is equally measured and thoroughly scanned. The measurement and scanning of the ruling party, on the one hand, and the opposition on the other, helps a great deal in the expression of public opinion through the ballot box. In a competent multi-party system or bi-party system there is always a periodic shift from one political party to the other or from one political authority to the other, when the actions of Government are totally different from that of demands and aspirations of the general public. The general elections serve the basic purpose of the periodic shift in the political elite.[11]

(C) General Elections in India

The General elections was held for the first time in 1951. However, then the House had a strength of 489 seats, with members chosen from the 26 states of India. Presently, there are total of 545 members in the House, with two unelected members as representatives of the Anglo-Indian community in India. A total of 543 members are chosen by the general elections.

The General election continues to be the most important political event in the country. They are held once in every five year, unless the Central government is dissolved beforehand. India follows a bicameral legislative structure. The members to the House of the People or the Lok-Sabha are elected through the General elections. These members are chosen from the parliamentary constituencies. The number of parliamentary

---

[10] Ramshray, Roy. The Uncertain Verdict. New Delhi: Orient Longman's Ltd., 1972. p.1

[11] . Ibid.

constituencies in a state depends upon the size and the population of the state. The executive along with the Council of Ministers is chosen from among the members of the winning party or the ruling coalition, as the case may be.

The State elections in India are structurally similar to the general elections in India. It chooses members for the state assembly. The numbers of seats in the assembly as well as the number of members in the Cabinet vary from state to state, depending on its size and population.

(D) Types of elections

Basic to democratic polity is the concept of sovereign powers vesting in the "people". In modern democracies, the people govern themselves through their elected representatives. In a parliamentary system, the executive comes out of the legislature and remains part of it and responsible to it. The election of members to the houses of legislatures is conducted through an institutionalized electoral process. This electoral process therefore, no matter how it is designed and conducted, forms the foundation of a parliamentary democracy. Elections are critical to the maintenance and development of democratic tradition because at one level, these are influenced by the political culture in which they operate, but at another, they also generate strong influences that can improve or distort this political culture. As a representative parliamentary democracy, India has a well-established system of direct and indirect elections to maintain its institutions. This may be described briefly as follows:

1. Direct Elections

Of the two Houses of Parliament, the Lok-Sabha is directly elected from defined single member territorial constituencies under universal adult suffrage (above 18 years) and on the basis of first-past the post system (FPTP). Similarly, adult voters directly elect all State Legislative Assemblies from territorial constituencies within their respective States.

2. Indirect Elections

The constitutional Head of the State, the President of India, is indirectly elected by an electoral college. Other indirect elections elect the Vice-President, the Rajya-Sabha and the Legislative Councils at State level.

3. Elections to Local Bodies

Elections to the Panchayat Raj Institutions (PRIs) that have been made mandatory by the 73rd and 74th Amendments to the Constitution are governed by the constitutional provisions of Part IX and Part IX A (articles 243 to 243 ZG) and State laws on PRIs.(panchayat raj institutions)

All of these elections, except item 3 above, are under the supervision, direction and control of an independent constitutional body called the Election Commission of India (article 324). Elections under item 3 are under the supervision and control of the State Election Commissioners (article 243 K & 243 ZA),

(E) Need for reforms.

Every system needs to be updated, so is the case with electoral system. India as having distinction of being the world's largest democracy has been experiencing and conducting elections on a very large scale. The numerous voting behavior studies have shown elections as an integral part of democratic institutional arrangement. They came to be accepted by the people as the matter of center importance and are endowed with a great amount of legitimacy. The elections are also an important instrument for reflecting the hopes of people, and if these hopes are bypassed, again these elections stand for change. The major example of this type was first time witnessed by India in 1975 when Congress party imposed emergency and soon party lost elections badly when emergency was lifted.

But from past several years the public faith in electoral process is diminishing is due to increasing distortions in the electoral system. There is no doubt that, at present time, there exists a widespread feeling that the electoral system and the other processes of law associated with it must be revised so as to make them compatible with the spirit of free and fair representation.[12]

The process of maturing of India has been very slow. We are a very long way from attaining maturity as a democracy the placing of personal ambitions above those of the nation raise serious doubts about the efficiency of the system of parliamentary democracy. The public is greatly anguished and concerned at the utter debasement of

---

[12] Bhagat Anjana, kaw. <u>Elections and Electoral Reforms in India.</u> New Delhi: vikass publishing house pvt.ltd., 1996. p.7

politics in country. Barring exceptions, politicians command the least respect. They are shunned and hated. They are often ridiculed, they are generally considered self serving, unprincipled thugs, interested only in furthering their own nests as soon as they come to occupy positions of power and authority. They have utterly let down the interests of general public and the country at large.

If our country's democratic polity has to survive, true representative character of our legislature must be ensured. For this a mechanism must be evolved. A free and fair poll is essential for a truly representative government.[13]

Its urgently necessary to take care full , systematic and impartial stock of situation and come up with certain well thought-out recommendations for not only removing the defects that have crept into electoral system but also for devising an electoral system educate enough to resist the tendency towards degeneration.[14]

2 CONSTITUTIONAL POSITIONS

(A)Election commission of India/establishment

Democracy advocates democratically elected governments which are responsible to elected parliament and state

[13]R, Meenu. Elections 1998 A continuity in Coalition. New Delhi: National Publishing, 1998. p.247
[14]Bhagat Anjana, kaw. Elections and Electoral Reforms in India. New Delhi: vikass publishing house pvt.ltd., 1996. p.15

legislature. Free and fare elections are forming the bed rock for all democratically elected governing bodies. Therefore the, constitution of India has given due importance to this aspect of free and fare elections by developing a separate part (part xv) to elections. To carry out the constitutional mandate of free and fare elections, the constitution created an independent constitutional authority, the election commission of India, to conduct elections to the offices of president, vice president and to the parliament and state legislature. (realizing the importance of free and fare elections even to Panchayats and Municipalities, parliament amended the constitution in 1992 to create a similar independent constitutional authority, state election commission for each state to conduct elections to panchayats and municipalities.)[15]

The framers of Indian constitution gave careful and earnest consideration for setting up an independent election authority. The constitution provides for a one man commission namely the chief election commissioner, permanently in office. The constitution has ensured that this officer shall perform his duties uninfluenced by the party political considerations and free from executive interference. The chief election commissioner cannot be removed from his office except in like manner and on like grounds as a judge of the Supreme Court. His conditions of service cannot be varied to hid disadvantage after his appointment.[16] (Article 324: Clause 5).

The conduct of elections in India after independence became the responsibility of the Election Commission. It was in 1950 that the Election Commission of India was set up as a constitutional body and entrusted with the task of superintendence, direction and control of all national and state level elections. It was also given the work of preparation and revision of electoral rolls. The Constitution has provision for a single election commissioner to manage elections for both Parliament and the state legislatures. There was much discussion in the Constituent Assembly regarding the set-ting up of a single body to handle elections at both the levels. Some members of the Constituent Assembly saw this as a move towards an uncalled for centralization, but the proposal was carried forth. The election commissioner has "considerable autonomy of action" as it derives its authority directly from the Constitution. To enable the election commissioner to work in a

[15]Fadia, B.L. Indian Government and Politics. Agra: Sahitiya Bhawan, 2013. P.670

[16]Bhagat Anjana, kaw. Elections and Electoral Reforms in India. New Delhi: vikass publishing house pvt.ltd., 1996. pp.24-25

reasonably autonomous manner without undue interference from the government, a pro-vision was made that "the chief election commissioner shall not be removed from his office except in like manner and on the like grounds as a judge of the Supreme Court", and that his conditions of service would not be altered to his disadvantage after he took over as the chief election commissioner (Article 324: Clause 5). The EC was also vested with residuary powers by the Supreme Court to take decisions on its own issues where the enacted laws were silent or the provisions were inadequate to handle any electoral matter. Provisions were incorporated in the Constitution that Parliament would, from time to time, make laws that would help the election commissioner in conducting elections. Two major laws were framed just after India became a republic - these were the Representation of the People Act, 1950, and the Representation of the People Act, 1951. The first deals with the allocation of seats, the delimitation of parliamentary and assembly constituencies, the preparation and revision of electoral rolls, etc. The second contains provisions on all aspects of conduct of elections and post-election disputes. Changes have been carried out in these laws over the years.[17]

(B) Composition of Election Commission.

The Election Commission consists of the Chief Election Commissioner and such number of Election Commissioners, if any, as the President may fix from time to time. The Chief Election Commissioner stands at the apex of the hierarchy of the Election Commission of India. All these commissioners are appointed by the President subject to the provisions of any law enacted by Parliament for the purpose. Indeed, the President appoints them at the behest of the Prime Minister because it is a constitutional necessity under the Parliamentary system of government which India has adopted. Chief Election Commissioner acts as the Chairman of the Election Commission in case any other Election Commissioner besides him is appointed.

To assist the Chief Election Commissioner in the performance of his onerous duties, there exists large paraphernalia of the officers and the staff subordinate to him. Among them are the Regional Commissioner, Deputy Election Commissioner, Secretary, Under Secretary, Research Officers etc.

To carry out its operations throughout the length and breadth of the

---

[17] Katju, Manjari. "Election Commission and Function of Democracy" Economic and Poetical Weekly. (apr 29-may5, 2006), vol.41 p.1635.

country, the Election Commission has to maintain election machinery at different rungs of the administration. At the state or the Union Territory level there is the Chief Electoral Officer as the king- pin in the electoral machinery. He is nominated by the Election Commission in consultation with the State/UT (union territory) Government. He is usually a senior executive or judicial officer of the State Government. He is assisted by the joint, deputy or assistant Chief Electoral Officers as well as the rest of the staff appointed by him in consultation with the State Government. At the district level the electoral duties are discharged by the District Officer or the Executive officer in addition to his normal administration routine. He was accorded statutory status only in 1966 through an amendment to the Representation of the People's Act, 1950. The responsibility for the preparation and revision of electoral rolls is vested in an officer called the Electoral Registration Officer. He may have under him Assistant Electoral Registration Officers. The Officers of the status of deputy collectors' such as sub-divisional officer and executive officers of large municipal corporations are designated as electoral registration officers and revenue officers junior to them such as Tehsildars are nominated as assistant electoral registration officers.

The election in every constituency is supervised by an officer known as the Returning Officer nominated by the Election Commission in consultation with the government of the state. The same officer can be nominated as Returning Officer for more than one constituency. He is assisted by one or more assistant Returning Officers so designated by the Election Commission. The Returning Officers for assembly constituencies' are usually drawn from the cadre of sub-divisional officers while those for Parliamentary Constituencies are district officers. The State government sends the list of officials with their designations to the Election Commission which after scrutinizing the same formally designates them as such for assembly and Parliamentary constituencies

The staff consisting of Presiding and Polling Officers, for the actual conduct of the poll is appointed by the District Election Officer. Prior to 1966, this was the responsibility of the Returning Officer. The District Election Officer may appoint a Presiding Officer for each polling station and such polling officer or officers are necessary. The presiding officer keeps order at the polling station and ensures the fair conduct of the poll. Usually government servants with some administrative capacity and some knowledge of the election law and reputation for integrity are, therefore picked up for appointment as presiding officers[18]

---

[18] Fadia, B.L. Reforming Election Commission. pp.79-81, 15 march 2014 <https:

(C), List of Officers

1. Chief Electoral Officer (CEO):

The election commission nominates or designates an officer of the government of a state or UT (union territory) to supervise the election work of the state or UT in consultation by the state or UT (union territory).

2. District Election Officer (DEO):

The election commission nominates or designates an officer of state government as the DEO in consultation with the state government. He is in control of CEO and supervises the election work of a district.

3. Returning Officer (RO):

The RO of a parliament or assembly constituency is responsible for the conduct of elections in the parliament or assembly constituency. The election commission of India nominates or designates an officer of the government or local authority as RO for each of the parliament or assembly constituencies in consultation with the state government or UT (union territory). The election commission may also appoint one or more assistant ROs to assist RO.

4. Electoral Registration Officer (ERO):

The ERO of a parliament or assembly constituency is responsible for preparation or revision of electoral rolls. The election commission of India nominates or designates an officer of the government or local authority as ERO for each of the parliament or assembly constituencies in consultation with the state government or UT (union territory). The election commission may also appoint one or more assistant EROs to assist ERO.

5. Presiding Officer:

These presiding officers are appointed by the DEO and by RO in case of a UT (union territory). These along with the polling officers, appointed

//www.jstore.org/stable41855597>

by the DEO/RO shall assist presiding officer to conduct polls at a polling station.

6. **Observers:**

The election commission of India appoints observers from government for parliament and assembly constituencies. Observers may be of two types: General observers and election expenditure observers. They perform functions as asked by the commission and directly report to the commission.[19]

(D) Functions and Powers of the Election Commission

The Election Commission of India has to perform multifarious duties assigned to it under the Constitution. Some of the principal functions of the Commission are:

1. **Demarcation of Constituencies**

To facilitate the process of elections a country has to be divided into several constituencies. The task of delimiting the constituencies is generally performed by a delimitation commission. But the power to delimit parliamentary and assembly constituencies for the first general elections in 1951 was conferred on the President. The President's delimitation order was to be released on the advice of the Election Commission which also consulted Parliamentary Advisory Committees set by the Speaker of Parliament and the Speaker of the respective legislative assembly to which the delimitation proposals pertained. The Election Commission distributed the seats district wise in each one of the States and directed the Chief Electoral Officers to prepare proposals for the physical demarcation of Constituencies according to the prescribed criteria. The procedure adopted in the delimitation of constituencies in 1951 led to a virtual power in the hands of the ruling party to decide about the contours of the Constituencies as it suited its designs. The association of Parliamentary Advisory Committees with the delimitation Commission mission gave top priority to political considerations. The election commission strongly pleaded for taking away this power from the Parliament. As an outcome of the recommendation of the Election Commission, the Parliament enacted the Delimitation Act, 1952. The Delimitation Commission was to consist of three members, two of whom

---

[19] 15 march 2014 <http://www.erewise.com/current-affairs/elections-and-electoral-reforms-in- india _art52c136657625a.html#.Uxy1T_mSzL4>

were to be nominated by the President from serving or retired judges of the Supreme Court or High Courts while the Chief Election Commissioner was to be an ex- officio member.

2. Electoral Rolls.

The second important but tedious function of the Election Commission is to prepare for identification, the up-to date list of all the persons who are entitled for voting at the poll.

3. Recognition of Political Parties and Allotment of Symbols.

Another important function of the Election Commission is to allot symbols to the political parties and the candidates, and also to accord recognition to the political parties. The Commission has specified certain symbols as reserved and others as free. The reserved symbols are only available for candidates sponsored by the political parties and the free symbols are equally available to other candidates. The Election Commission has power to adjudicate upon disputes with regard to recognition of political parties and rival claims to a particular symbol for purposes of elections.

4. Scrutiny of the Nomination Papers.

Another function of the Election Commission is to examine the nomination papers of the candidates. These papers are accepted if found in order, but rejected otherwise. This duty is performed by the Returning officer who notified to all the contesting candidates the date, time and place for the formal scrutiny of nomination papers.

The Returning Officer summarily but judicially examines all the nomination papers and decides the objections rose. He is also to see whether the requisite requirements of security deposit, election symbol, election agent etc. have also been fulfilled. He is empowered to reject the nomination papers either by upholding the objection raised by a rival candidate or on his own motion or any of the following grounds:

(a) that the candidate either is not qualified or is disqualified to fill the seat under any of the relevant constitutional provisions, viz. Articles 84, 102, 173 and 191,

(b) That the provisions of Sections 33 and 34 of the Representation of the people Act, 1951 have not been complied ' with; and

(c) That the signature of the candidate or the proposer on the nomination papers is not genuine.

5. The Conduct of the Poll.

Another stupendous task that the Election Commission has to undertake is the conduct of the poll throughout the whole of India. In a Parliamentary or Assembly constituency, the Returning Officer is to make suitable arrangement for conducting the poll with the prior approval of the Election Commission. The Commission can order a re-poll for the whole constituency under compulsion of circumstances. Article 324 confers on the Election Commission necessary powers to conduct the elections including the power to countermand the poll in a constituency and ordering a fresh poll therein because of hooliganism and breakdown of law and order at the time of polling or counting of votes.

6. Election Expenses.

Another most controversial function that the Election Com- mission has to perform is to scrutinize the accounts of election expenses submitted by contestants in elections. In India every contesting candidate is required to maintain and file the accounts of his election expenses within a prescribed period after the publication of the result of his election. Within 10 days from the last date of filing the returns, the Returning Officer submits to the Election Commission a list of all the candidates and their agents together with their returns as also his observation in respect of candidates who have failed to lodge returns in the specified time and in accordance with the procedure prescribed by law. The Commission scrutinizes the accounts and decides whether the returns are in proper form and whether they have been lodged in time. In case of default it notifies the candidates or their agents of their disqualification by publishing these in the Official Gazette.[20]

7. Advisory and quasi judicial functions.

Under the constitution, the commission has advisory jurisdiction in the matter of post elections disqualification of sitting members of parliament and state legislatures. Further the case of person found guilty of corrupt practices at elections which come before the supreme court and high courts are also referred to commission for its opinion on the question as to whether such person shall be disqualified and, if so, for what period.

---

[20] Fadia, B.L. Reforming Election Commission. pp.81-83. 15 march 2014 <https://www.jstore.org/stable41855597>

The opinion of the commission in all such matters is binding on the president or, as the case may be, the governor to whom such opinion is tendered. The commission has the power to disqualify a candidate who has failed to lodge an account of his election expenses within the time and in the manner prescribed by law. The commission has also the power for removing of reducing the period of such disqualification as other disqualification.

8. Judicial review

The decisions of the commission can be challenged in the high court and the supreme court of India by appropriate petitions. By a long standing convection and several judicial pronouncements, once the actual process of election has started, the judiciary does not intervene in the actual conduct of polls. Once the poll is completed and the result declared, the commission cannot review any result on its own. This can only be reviewed through the process of an evection petition, which can be filed before the high court, in respect of elections to the parliament and state legislatures. In respect of election for the office of the president and vice president, such petitions can only be filed before the supreme court of India.

9. Media policy.

The commission has a comprehensive policy for the media. It holds regular briefings for the mass media print and electronic, on a regular base, at close intervals during the election period and on the specific occasion. The representatives of media are also provided facilities to report on actual conduct of poll and counting. They are allowed the entry in to polling stations and counting centers on the basis of authority letters issued by the commission. They include members of both national and international media. The commission also publishes the the statistical reports and other documents which are available in the public domain. The library of commission is available for research and study to members of academic fraternity; media representatives and anybody else interested. The commission is in cooperation with state owned media Doordarshan and all India radio.

10. International co-operation.

India is a founding member of international institute for Democracy and Electoral Assistance (IDEA), Stockholm Sweden, in the recent past, the commission has expanded international contacts by the way of sharing of experience and expertise in the areas of Electoral Management and

Administration, Electoral laws and Reforms. Delegates of commission have visited several countries – Russia, Sri lanka, Nepal, Indonesia, south Africa, Bangladesh, Thailand. Nigeria, Australia, the united states of Afghanistan, have visited the commission for a better understanding of Indian electoral process. The commission has also provided experts and observes for elections to other countries in co-operation with United Nations and Commonwealth Secretariat.

11. New initiatives.

The commission has taken several new initiatives in the recent past. Notable among these are, a scheme for use of state owned electronic media for broadcast/telecast by political parties, checking criminalization of politics, computerization of electoral rolls with identity cards, simplifying the procedure for maintenance of accounts and filling of the same by candidate and variety of the measures for strict compliance of Model Code of Conduct, for proving a level playing field to contest elections.[21]

(E) List of articles of constitution dealing with elections

Articles from 324 to 329 in part XV of the Indian constitution deals with elections, they say;

Article 324:

Superintendence, direction and control of elections to be vested in an election commission.
(1) The superintendence, direction and control of the preparation of the electoral rolls, conduct elections to the parliament and every state legislature and offices of president and vice president.

(2) The elections are conducted by a chief election commissioner and such number of other election commissioners, if any as the president may time for time fix. Their appointment is subjected to law made in that behalf by parliament.

---

[21] Fadia, B.L. Indian Government and Politics. Delhi: Sahitya Bhawan, 2013. pp. 678-679

(3) If any of so election commissioners is appointed, chief election commissioner shall act as chairman of election commission.

(4) Before any election in India (Elections to parliament, legislative assemblies, legislative councils, general elections or biennial elections), the president after consulting chief election commissioner may appoint regional commissioners to assist election commission.

(5) The conditions of service and tenure of election commissioners and regional commissioners are like they shall not be removed from office except in manner and grounds for removal of Supreme Court chief justice and they shall be removed without the recommendation of chief election commissioner.

(6) The president or the governor shall provide adequate staff to election commission if requested to discharge functions of elections.

Article 325:

No person shall be ineligible for inclusion in, or to claim to be included in a special electoral roll on grounds of religion, race, caste or sex.
There shall be no special provision or representation for anyone. One general electoral roll for a territorial constituency and no person shall be excluded on the grounds mentioned.

Article 326:

Elections to the House of the people and to the legislative assemblies of states to be on the basis of adult suffrage
Every person, who is citizen of India and who is not less than 18 years of age on the date of elections can cast vote to general elections of parliament or state assemblies or biennial elections. The person can only be disqualified on grounds of unsound mind, non residence, crime or corrupt or illegal practices.

Article 327:

Power of parliament to make provisions with respect to elections to legislatures

Power of parliament to make provision with respect to all matters relating to elections. The provisions may be like delimitation of constituencies, electoral rolls etc.

Article 328:

Power of legislature of state to make provision with respect to elections to such legislature

If a state feels few or more provisions are not made by parliament, then, legislature of a state has power to make provision with respect to all matters relating to elections. The provision may be like delimitation of constituencies, electoral rolls etc.

Article 329:

Bar to interference by courts in electoral matters.

(a) The validity of any law made due respect of elections under article 327 and article 328 cannot be questioned in any court.

(b) No election shall be questioned except by an election petition presented to concerned authority.

(E) Exceptional cases and points to remember:

- Though the powers of election commission are wide, they cannot violate the provisions of any law including state acts. But precautionary measures are not illegal.
- No election can be invalidated on the ground that the electoral officer failed to comply with the non-statutory directions issued by the commission though the electoral officer is binding on the directions.
- Bar of article 329(a) will not come into play when case falls under articles 191 and 193 and whole of the election process is over.
- Parliament has enacted the Representation of the Peoples Acts 1950, 1951 and the Delimitation commission Acts 1952, 1962, 1972(repealed), 2002, 2003 to prescribe the mode of election, and the formation and delimitation of the constituencies relating to election.
- The election commission of India is a three member body now.[22]

(F) Conclusion

The working and deepening of democracy in India has enhanced the role of the election commission and has given it a position of importance almost at par with the executive, the legislature and the judiciary. The election commission, trusted by the electorate, has been so far, able to perform its enhanced role fairly well. Its performance shows that it has more or less encouraged the growth of democratic aspirations, despite the fact that the unfolding of these aspirations is happening in an "untidy" manner. It has also tried to ensure that democratic ambitions play themselves out in an environment of rules and norms where the under-privileged do not trample upon each other and do not get trampled upon by the powerful. In this role of an umpire it has tried to control the use of money and muscle power and the ruling-party arbitrariness. However, what needs to be emphasized here is that the nature of its actions has been largely ad hoc. Decisions have been taken by the election commission through on the spot assessments of the situations. Though these decisions have been largely fair, this ad hoc manner of functioning can take the election commission in the opposite direction of the surging democratic tide. Therefore, this ad hoc manner of working needs to be replaced by a more thought out and informed stance on the needs of the electorate and the democratic system' in India. The election commission has to ensure that politicization happens, that it remains within the boundaries of democratic norms, and that these norms themselves do not rest unequally on the contesting sides and lead to de-politicization of the weak. A long-term strategy or a conscious policy needs to be developed where the growth of democratic aspirations goes together with rule enforcement. This is essential for strengthening democratic values and handling the jolts and unexpected problems that might come up.[23]

---

[22]15 march 2014 <http://www.erewise.com/current-affairs/elections-and-electoral-reforms-in-india_art52c136657625a.html#.Uxy1T_mSzL4>
[23] Katju, manjari. Election Commission and Functioning of Democracy. p.1639. 15 march 2014 <https://www.jstore.org/stable/4418140>

3 MAJOR ELECTORAL REFORMS IN INDIA

Major Electoral Reforms in India

Elections are one of the most important features of the democratic process which constitutes the sign post of democracy. It grants people a government and the government has constitutional right to govern those who elect it. Elections provide an opportunity to the people to express their faith in the government from time to time and change it when the need arises. Elections symbolize the sovereignty of the people and provide legitimacy to the authority of the government. Thus, free and fair elections are indispensable for the success of democracy. In a democratic country like India, people have the real power and choice to elect their representatives. By this only the real welfare state will arise. Because now a-days people all over the world want welfare state only.[24]

India is a vast country with a population of 1.22 billion as per 2011 census. It has 28 states and 7 union territories with 545 constituencies for elections to central legislature and more than 5200 constituencies to state legislatures. So far, elections to Lok Sabha (House of People) were held 15 times, the last being held in 2009. Even in the first elections of independent India (1951-52), there were 489 voting constituencies for Lok sabha and 5,283 constituencies of state legislatures. In the 1951-52 elections, there were 1,800 candidates contested for 489 seats of Lok Sabha and 15000 candidates for 5283 seats of states legislatures. During the first and second general elections, polls to the central and state legislatures were simultaneously held. In all later elections the elections to several state legislatures followed a time schedule different from national elections. In addition there are always some by elections in one part of the country or other. The above facts show the gigantic nature of Indian election process. The successful conduct of elections since 1952, in spite of very serious difficulties, is a proof that democracy has taken deep roots in India. Till a few decades ago, India was considered to be a under developed country with a huge illiterates, rural oriented tradition-bound and Caste-ridden population. Vast distances involved the inaccessible terrain in several constituencies, problems of mobilizing sufficient staff for election duty and providing security—all these are major obstacles for conducting free and fair elections. However, the election commission gained a wide knowledge of difficulties of conducting elections year by year after conducting several Lok Sabha and State Assembly elections.

Electoral Reforms

People observed serious malpractices in elections and there was criticism in the parliament and by the press and intelligentsia. The election commission also realized the necessity of urgent reforms. The Government has appointed committees like Justice Tarkunde Committee (1975) and Dinesh Goswami Committee (1990) recommended extensive electoral reforms. The reforms have considerably transformed the election process. Some of the important legislative resolutions pertaining

---

[24] Rao Pedamalla Sreenivasa, Mohammad.Masliuddin. Electoral Reforms and Leg islative Resolutions in a Big Democratic India: An Analysis. p.36. 1 may 2014 <fi le:///C:/Users/indore/Downloads/3334-5371-1-PB%20(1).pdf>

to the electoral reforms are discussed below:[25]

A. Constitution (61st amendment) Act 1988

The Sixty-first Amendment of the Constitution of India, officially known as The Constitution (Sixty-first Amendment) Act, 1988, lowered the voting age of elections to the Lok Sabha and to the Legislative Assemblies of States from 21 years to 18 years. This was done by amending Article 326 of the Constitution, which related to elections to the Lok Sabha and the Assemblies.

The bill of The Constitution (Sixty-first Amendment) Act, 1988 was introduced in the Lok Sabha on 13 December 1988, as the Constitution (Sixty-second Amendment) Bill, 1988 (Bill No. 129 of 1988). It was introduced by B. Shankaranand, then Minister of Water Resources. The bill sought to amend Article 326 of the Constitution, relating to elections to the Lok Sabha and to the Legislative Assemblies of States based on adult suffrage. The full text of the Statement of Objects and Reasons appended to the bill is given below:

Article 326 of the Constitution provides that the elections to the House of the People and to the Legislative Assembly of every State shall be on the basis of adult suffrage, that is to say, a person should not be less than 21 years of age. It has been found that many of the countries have specified 18 years as the voting age. In our country some of the State Governments have adopted 18 years of age for elections to the local authorities. The present-day youth are literate and enlightened and the lowering of the voting age would provide to the unrepresented youth of the country an opportunity to give vent to their feelings and help them become a part of the political process. The present-day youth are very much politically conscious. It is, therefore, proposed to reduce the voting age from 21 years to 18 years.[26]

The bill was debated by the Lok Sabha on 14 and 15 December 1988, and was passed on 15 December, after adopting a formal amendment to replace the word "Sixty-second" with "Sixty-first" in Clause 1 of the bill. The Rajya Sabha debated the bill on 16, 19 and 20 December 1988 and passed it on 20 December 1988, after adopting the amendment made by the Lok Sabha. The bill, after ratification by the States, received assent

---

[25] ibid p.37-38

[26] 25 april 2014 < http://en.wikipedia.org/wiki/Sixty-first_Amendment_of_the_Constitution_of_India >

from then President Ramaswamy Venkataraman on 28 March 1989. It was notified in The Gazette of India, and also came into force on the same date[27]

The following is actual specimen of bill[28]

---

[27] ibid

[28] 25 april 2014 <http://indiacode.nic.in/coiweb/amend/amend61.htm>

THE CONSTITUTION (SIXTY-FIRST AMENDMENT) ACT, 1988
Statement of Objects and Reasons appended to the Constitution (Sixty-second Amendment) Bill, 1988 (Bill No. 129 of 1988) which was

enacted as THE CONSTITUTION (Sixty-first Amendment) Act, 1988

STATEMENT OF OBJECTS AND REASONS

Article 326 of the Constitution provides that the elections to the House of the People and to the Legislative Assembly of every State shall be on the basis of adult suffrage, that is to say, a person should not be less than 21 years of age. It has been found that many of the countries have specified 18 years as the voting age. In our country some of the State Governments have adopted 18 years of age for

elections to the local authorities. The present-day youth are literate and enlightened and the lowering of the voting age would provide to the unrepresented youth of the country an opportunity to give vent to their feelings and help them become a part of the political process. The present-day youth are very much politically conscious. It is, therefore, proposed to reduce the voting age from 21 years to 18 years.

2. The Bill seeks to achieve the above object.

NEW DELH

B SHANKARANAND.

The 9th December, 1988.
 THE CONSTITUTION (SIXTY-FIRST AMENDMENT ACT, 1988)
[28th March, 1989.]
An Act further to amend the Constitution of India.
BE it enacted by Parliament in the Thirty-ninth Year of the Republic of India as follows:-
1. Short title.- This Act may be called the Constitution (Sixty-first Amendment) Act, 1988.
2. Amendment of article 326.-In article 326 of the Constitution, for the words "twenty-one years", the words "eighteen years" shall be substituted.

B. Representation of Peoples' Act (Amendment) 1996 (Amendments became effective from 1-8-1996)

a) Any Conviction under section 2 (Insulting Indian National Flag or Constitution of India) or Section 3 (preventing of singing National Anthem) of the "Prevention of insults to national honour Act 1971" will entail disqualification for a period of six years from contesting to parliament or state legislatures.

b) Amount of security deposit for contesting to Parliament is enhanced from Rs. 500/- to Rs. 10,000/- (in case of S.C/S.T candidates from Rs.250/- to Rs.5, 000/- only). The security deposit for contesting to state legislatures is enhanced from Rs.250/- to Rs, 5,000/- (In case of SC/ST candidates from Rs.125/- to Rs. 2500/- only). This is done to discourage non-serious candidates and to reduce multi cornered contests.

c) An independent candidate contesting for Parliament or Assembly has to be proposed by at least 10 persons of the constituency. In case of candidate of a recognized party only one proposer is sufficient.

d) Interval between last date of withdrawal and date of poll is reduced from 20 days to 14 days.

e) A candidate shall not contest for more than two constituencies (either parliamentary or assembly constituencies). The same restrictions apply to by-elections to House of People/State Assembly and also to biennial elections to Rajya Sabha and State Legislative Councils.

f) Elections will not be countermanded on the death of a candidate. If the deceased candidate was put up by a recognized national or state party, an alternative candidate can be nominated within 7 days of issue of notice by the election commission about such death.

g) Carrying fire arms (as defined in Arms act 1959) within neighborhood of the polling stations is a cognizable offence punishable with imprisonment up to 2 years or fine or both. Such fire arms will be confiscated and license will be revoked. These provisions will not apply to authorized police officers and election officers on duty.

h) Sale or distribution of liquor within the polling area is punishable with imprisonment for six months or with fine up to Rs. 2000/- or both.

i) Bye elections to Parliament or state legislature will be held within 6 months of occurrence of a vacancy. However, if remainder of the term is less than 6 months or if election commission, in consultation with government, feels that it is difficult to hold elections for any other reason, then bye-election will not be held. The vacancy will be filled only in the next regular elections.[29]

C. The Presidential and Vice-Presidential Elections (Amendment) Ordinance 1997

It is increased number of proposers and seconderers to 50 each in place of ten for each presidential candidate. It increased proposers and seconderers to 20 each in place of 5 for each vice presidential candidate. For election to both the offices the security deposit was increased to Rs. 15,000/- from Rs. 25,000/-

D. Section 60 of Representation of Peoples Act 1951

A sub section was inserted for providing facility of postal ballot to certain sections of people in addition to existing categories like Armed forces personnel. The provision was meant to facilitate right of franchise to migrants from Kashmir Valley for general election to 12th Lok Sabha.[30]

E. Section 61 A of Representation of Peoples Act 1951: (w.e.f. 15-3-1998)

Election Commission of India to make reforms in the electoral process to ensure free and fair elections. EVMs, devised and designed by Election Commission of India in collaboration with two Public Sector undertakings viz., Bharat Electronics Limited, Bangalore and Electronics Corporation of India Limited, Hyderabad, is a major step

---

[29]Rao Pedamalla Sreenivasa, Mohammad. Masliuddin. Electoral Reforms and Leg islative Resolutions in a Big Democratic India: An Analysis. P.39. 1 may 2014< fi le:///C:/Users/indore/Downloads/3334-5371-1-PB%20(1).pdf >
[30] ibid pg. no. 39

in this direction[31]

Initial use of Electronic Voting Machines

These machines were used for the first time during the general elections to the Kerala Legislative Assembly held in May 1982. To start with, Electronic Voting Machines were used in 50 polling stations of Parur assembly constituency In Kerala. Thereafter, these machines were used in 1982-83 in 10 other constituencies spread over 8 States in different parts of the country, including some difficult areas in the North-East. The number of polling stations involved ranged from 12 to 159. It was found that voting by means of these machines was quite simple and much faster than the conventional system. Counting was also very easy and hassle free.[32]

Salient Features of EVMs

1 It is tamper proof & simple to operate
2 Program which controls the functioning of the control unit is burnt into a micro chip on a "one time programmable basis". Once burnt it cannot be read, copied out or altered.
3 Eliminates the possibility of invalid votes makes the counting process faster and reduces the cost of printing.
4 An EVM can be used in areas without electricity as it runs on alkaline batteries.5 Elections can be conducted through EVMs if the number of candidates does not exceed 64.
6 An EVM can record a maximum number of 3840 votes. [33]

Amendment to Law

On recommendation of the Election Commission, Parliament in December 1988 amended the Representation of the People Act, 1951 to provide for the use of Electronic Voting Machines. The amended provision, by way of a new section - 61-A, come into force with effect from 15th March, 1989. The relevant section is quoted below:

---

[31]26April2014<http://pibmumbai.gov.in/English/PDF/E2014_FR17.PDF>

[32]26 April 2014 <http://eci.nic.in/eci_main/eci_publications/books/miscell/elections-india.pdf>

[33] 26 April 2014 <http://pibmumbai.gov.in/English/PDF/E2014_FR17.PDF>

"61A, Voting machines at elections. — Notwithstanding anything contained in this Act or the rules made there under, the giving and recording of votes by voting machines in such manner as may be prescribed, may be adopted in such constituency or constituencies as the Election Commission may, having regard to the circumstances of each case, specify.

Explanation –

For the purpose of this section,

"Voting machine' means any machine or apparatus whether operated electronically or otherwise used for giving or recording of votes and any reference to a ballot box or ballot paper in this Act or the rules made there under shall, save as otherwise provided, be construed as including a reference to such voting machine wherever such voting machine is used at any election."

Amendments of Conduct of Elections Rules

In pursuance of the above amendment to the Representation of the People Act, 1951, the Central Government, in consultation with the Election Commission also amended the Conduct of Elections Rules, 1961 through its notification dated 24th March, 1992, by inserting a new Chapter II in Part IV (Rule 49 A to 49 X) for facilitating the use of Electronic Voting Machines.

Finalization of Design

Meanwhile, the Commission had been in constant interaction with the two Central Government undertakings, namely, Electronics Corporation of India Limited, Hyderabad (ECIL) and Bharat Electronics Limited, Bangalore (BEL) for improvement of the design and provision of additional facilities in the EVMs in the light of the experience gained at the elections in which the machines were used in 1982-83. The Commission ultimately finalized the design and model of the existing EVMs in May 1989[34]

Historic Decision to use EVMs

---

[34] 26April2014 <http://eci.nic.in/eci_main/eci_publications/books/miscell/elections-india.pdf >

Finally, the Commission took a historic decision to go ahead and start use of EVMs for assembly constituencies in November 1998. For this purpose, after detailed review of all relevant factors, the Commission selected 16 assembly constituencies spread over three states — Madhya Pradesh, Rajasthan and NCT of Delhi. These constituencies were carefully chosen on the basis of their compact urban character and good literacy and adequate infrastructure to manage the logistics for introducing EVMs for elections.[35]

F. Act I of 1989 (Amending to Section 58 of Representation of Peoples Act 1951)

This amendment provides for adjournment of poll or countermanding in case of booth capturing. The definition of booth capturing was given in Representation of Peoples Act (RPA) 1951. It includes:

a) Forcing polling officers to surrender ballot boxes, EVMs etc.

b) Ensuring that only a certain candidate's supporter vote and others cannot vote.

c) Threatening of voters, not to go to polling stations.

d) Seizure of ballot papers, EVMs etc and seizure of the place of counting itself.

e) Convenience of officials with candidates in booth capturing in any of the above methods.

f) Section 135A provides for jail term of 6 months to 2 years along with fine. If such offence is committed by government official he is punishable with imprisonment of 1 to 3 years along with fine.
 Disclosing of particulars of convictions/punishments and assets and liabilities by contesting candidates.[36]

---

[35] ibid
[36] Rao Pedamalla Sreenivasa, Mohammad. Masliuddin. Electoral Reforms and Legislative Resolutions in a Big Democratic India: An Analysis. P.40. 1 may 2014 < file:///C:/Users/indore/Downloads/3334-5371-1-PB%20(1).pdf>

G. Representation of Peoples Act (III Amendment) Act 2002

It amended Representation of Peoples Act 1951 and as a result the following changes were brought about:

a) The candidate for Parliament or State Legislature has to disclose

(1) whether he was accused of any offence punishable with conviction for 2 years or more in a case in which charges were already framed, or

(2) Whether he was convicted for one year or more for any offence and whether punishment has been awarded.

b) Every candidate for Parliament and assembly elections has to declare before the presiding officer of parliament (I.e, speaker) the assets and liabilities of himself and also his spouse and dependent children.

c) He will be liable to be punished as for a criminal offence if he furnished any wrong affidavit. He would also be punished for furnishing any false information in nomination papers.

H. Representation of Peoples Act (Amendment) Act 2003

The punishments for above irregularities are given in the amended section 8 of RPA Act 1951. They are:

(a) Conviction plus disqualification for 6 years, or

(b) Fine plus disqualification for 6 years. Hereafter a person who is already serving a prison term cannot contest elections to Parliament and State Legislatures. Candidates (both for parliament and State elections) have to disclose the fact whether they have been charged with offences punishable by imprisonment of 2 years or more. If they are elected, they have to declare their assets and Liabilities to presiding officers.

I. Right to know the antecedents of candidates-The judicial dicta

In March 2003, the Supreme Court declared certain provisions in Representation of Peoples Act (III Amendment) Act 2002 (Section 33b) as null and void. The provisions which were struck down are as under: Section 33(b) of Representation of Peoples Act, (RPA) (amendment) Act 2002 states that "Notwithstanding anything contained in any judgment of any court or any order of EC, no candidate shall be liable to disclose or furnish any information, in respect of his election, which is not required to be disclosed or furnished under the Act or rules made there under". The court held that voters have a fundamental right to know the antecedents of a candidate to enable them to vote intelligently and that therefore the section 33(b) is in violation of fundamental rights of a citizen. As a result the Election Commission issued fresh guidelines regarding section 33-b of Representation of Peoples Act, 2002: The guidelines state that:

i) Failure of candidates to furnish in an affidavit their antecedents including any criminal record is violative of Supreme Court order of March 2003. In such circumstances the Returning officer is free to reject the nomination papers not accompanied by required affidavit.

ii) Every candidate is to file an affidavit along with nomination papers whether any case is pending against him in courts and if so details of the case, the movable and immovable assets owned by candidate or his dependents, his/her liabilities to public financial institutions and government dues and his educational qualifications.

iii) Such affidavit should be sworn before a 1st class Magistrate or Notary Public or Commissioner appointed by High Court.

iv)The information furnished by each candidate will be supplied to the respective returning officer who will display a copy in his office notice board and also supply copied of such affidavits to other candidates and also representatives of media[37]

J. Anti-defection law: Constitution (52nd Amendment) 1985

The Tenth Schedule — popularly known as the Anti-Defection Act — was included in the Constitution in 1985 by the Rajiv Gandhi ministry and sets the provisions for disqualification of elected members on the grounds of defection to another political party.

The law was added via the 52nd Amendment Act, 1985, soon after the Rajiv government came to power with a thumping majority in the wake of the assassination of Prime Minister Indira Gandhi. The Congress had won 401 seats in the Lok Sabha.

•What are the grounds for disqualification under the Anti-Defection Law's Articles 102 (2) and 191 (2)?

a) If an elected member voluntarily gives up his membership of a political party;

---

[37] Ibid. pp.40-41

b) If he votes or abstains from voting in such House contrary to any direction issued by his political party or anyone authorized to do so, without obtaining prior permission.

As a pre-condition for his disqualification, his abstention from voting should not be condoned by his party or the authorized person within 15 days of such incident.

What were the loopholes?

As per the 1985 Act, a 'defection' by one-third of the elected members of a political party was considered a 'merger'. Such defections were not actionable against. The Dinesh Goswami Committee on Electoral Reforms, the Law Commission in its report on "Reform of Electoral Laws" and the National Commission to Review the Working of the Constitution (NCRWC) all recommended the deletion of the Tenth Schedule provision regarding exemption from disqualification in case of a split.

Finally the 91st Constitutional Amendment Act, 2003, changed this. So now at least two-thirds of the members of a party have to be in favour of a "merger" for it to have validity in the eyes of the law. "The merger of the original political party or a member of a House shall be deemed to have taken place if, and only if, not less than two-thirds of the members of the legislature party concerned have agreed to such merger," states the Tenth Schedule.[38]

Purpose of law

To discourage the practice of defection of members from one party to another after their election, the Constitution (Fifty-Second Amendment) Act, 1985 was enacted by the Parliament. The Amendment to Article 102(regarding Members of either Houses of Parliament) and 191 (regarding Members of state legislatures) seeks to put an end to the evil of political defections that undermines the basic principle of democracy. Amendment had been made in Article 191 to provide that a person shall be disqualified for being a member of the state Legislature if he is so disqualified under the Tenth Schedule.[39]

---

[38]Rajgopal, Krishan Das. Anti defection Law. 22 march2014 <http://archive.indi anexpress.com/news/antidefection-law/339606/>
[39]22 march 2014 <http://delhiassembly.nic.in/antidefection.htm>

The tenth schedule

The new Tenth Schedule added in the Constitution contains provisions as to disqualification on the ground of defection. The question whether a member has become subject to the disqualification will be decided by the presiding officer of the House. The Speaker/Chairperson has been empowered to make rules for giving effect to the provisions of the Schedule.

Section 16 of the Government of the National Capital Territory of Delhi, Act, 1991" provides for disqualification of Members of the Delhi Assembly on grounds of defection. In pursuance of the powers conferred under the provisions of the Tenth Schedule and the GNCT Act, the "Members of Delhi Legislative Assembly (Disqualification on Ground of Defection) Rules, 1996" was framed[40]

Grounds of disqualification:

1) Tenth Schedule of the Constitution of India provides that a member of Lok Sabha or Rajya Sabha or Legislative Assembly of Legislative Council (hereafter referred as ('Legislature') is disqualified for being a member of the House if:

(a) He voluntarily gives up the membership of the political party that gave him the Ticket ('original political party') to contest the election;

OR

(b) If he votes or abstains from voting in the House contrary to any direction issued by the original political party without obtaining the prior permission of the original political party and such voting has not been condoned by the original Political party with in fifteen days from the date of voting or abstention.

2) Thus, a member of Legislature is bound to follow the instructions of his original Political party in all matters that are put to vote in the House and will be disqualified, if he does not follow these instructions. However, he will be saved from disqualification if his original political party condones his action in violation of the direction within fifteen days of voting.

---

[40] ibid

3) Thus, the disqualification under ground (b) becomes effective only once a member has voted in the House (and not before) but the disqualification under ground (a) becomes effective as and when it is clear that the member has voluntarily given up the membership of the original political party.

(In the recent controversy surrounding the Yeddiyurappa government (there have been quite a few in the past – reference made here to the episode wherein a number of BJP legislators had met the governor of Karnataka and submitted a letter mentioning that they were withdrawing support from the government headed by Mr.Yeddiyurappa) the Karnataka High Court opined that the italicized phrase (voluntarily gives up) is broad enough in scope to cover situations wherein a member of the original political party claims (expressly or impliedly) that he will not vote in favor of the government led by the person who had been chosen by the original political party as the Chief Minister - this would lead to the inference of (giving up the membership of the original political party and) incurring disqualification.

4) Also, note that an independent member of Legislature becomes disqualified for being a member of the House if he joins any political party after election.

5) A nominated member of Legislature becomes disqualified for being a member of the House if he joins any political party after six months from the date of taking oath as a member of the Legislature.

6) The Chairman or the Speaker of the House has been authorized to makes a decision `on questions as to the disqualification of a member.

Exception

7) In a situation where in the original political party merges with another political party (not less than two-thirds of the members of Legislature belonging to the original political party agree to such merger) and a member of the original political party joins the new group (formed subsequent to the merger) or opts to function as a separate group (old group that may or may not maintain the identity of the older political party

8) Please note that prior to 91st Amendment of the Constitution of India (2003) a split in the original political party whereby one-thirds of the members of Legislature belonging to the original political party may form a separate group and this did not attract disqualification. However,

subsequent to the 91st amendment, this exception is no longer available.

To illustrate, party ABC merges with party XYZ. Now, a member of the Legislature belonging to party ABC

(i) Become a part of XYZ; or
(ii) Refuse to become a part of XYZ and opt to function as member of ABC thereby keeping the identity of ABC alive; or
(iii) Refuse to become a part of XYZ and opt to function as a separate group by the name of DEF

To illustrate, before this amendment came into force; 4 out of 12 members (viz. one-thirds) of Legislature (from the original political party) could split from the original political party (thereby forming a separate group) and support another party without incurring disqualification. However, after the Amendment (in view of point no 6) a separate group constituting one-thirds of the members of Legislature belonging to the original political party can exist (and will not incur disqualification) only if a merger (as explained above) precedes the formation of the separate group.[41]

K. Ceiling on candidate's election expenditure

As per Oct 2002 order of Election Commission, ceiling at different rates was put for election expenditure of candidates for central and state legislatures as follows:

i) For Lok Sabha elections in 22 states the ceiling is fixed as Rs. 25 lakhs. In smaller states the ceiling is from Rs. 14 lakhs to Rs. 22 lakhs (previously this ceiling for entire India was Rs. 5 lakh only.)

ii) For Lok Sabha elections in Union Territories the ceiling is between Rs. 10 Lakhs to Rs. 25 Lakhs (In Delhi it is Rs. 25 Lakhs).

iii) For assembly constituencies the ceiling is Rs. 5 lakhs to Rs. 10 lakhs depending on size of constituencies.

iv) The ceiling applies to expenditure by candidates or his supporters/relatives on behalf of the candidate.
v) Expenditure of the party for campaigning on behalf of the candidate is

---

[41]22 march 2014 <http://www.careerlauncher.com/lstcontent/plansuppliments /attachments/50/64/Anti-defection%20law.PDF>

also included in this ceiling. But it excluded the expenditure on travel of party leaders on behalf of the candidates. It also excludes the expenditure on campaign material.

vi) A register should be maintained showing expenditure by candidate on daily basis. The party should also maintain such a register showing expenditure on each candidate separately.[42]

L. Voting rights to NRI'S (Non-resident Indians)

Non-resident Indians (NRIs) can now cast votes in their home constituencies as the government has notified rules in this regard, fulfilling the longstanding demand of such people estimated to be 11 million. The rules make it clear that the NRIs would have to register as voters and be "physically present" with their passport on the polling day to exercise their franchise. There is no provision for postal balloting. "Every citizen of India staying in a foreign country, who has not acquired citizenship of a foreign country, and has completed 18 years of age as on January 1 of the year, can make an application for being registered in the roll for the constituency pertaining to the locality in which his place of residence in India as mentioned in the passport is located," said the notification prepared in consultation with the Election Commission. This meets the longstanding demands of the NRIs and fulfills the promise made by Prime Minister Manmohan Singh at last year's Pravasi Bharatiya Divas, an annual congregation of Indian Diaspora here. As per the law so far, the name of an NRI would be deleted from the voters' list if he or she did not stay at their residence in India for six months at a stretch. The NRI voters now can submit the application directly to the electoral registration officer of the constituency within which the place of residence is mentioned in the passport. The application can either be submitted directly or sent by post. According to the Representation of the People Act, once a person is registered as a voter, he automatically has a right to contest polls also. As per the Representation of the People (Amendment) Act, 2010, so far a person who has gone out of the country for business or employment should be treated as having moved out of that place. Mere ownership or possession of a building or other immovable property did not bestow on the owner, the residential qualification.

---

[42] Rao Pedamalla Sreenivasa, Mohammad. Masliuddin. Electoral Reforms and Le gislative Resolutions in a Big DemocraticIndia: An Analysis. p.42. 1 may 2014 <f ile:///C:/Users/indore/Downloads/3334-5371-1-PB%20(1).pdf>

There are a large number of citizens of India residing outside India due to various reasons. They have been persistently demanding for conferring those voting rights, the Amendment Act said. Though the issue had been receiving the attention of the government for quite some time, the demand could not be acceded to owing to certain "practical difficulties" in enrolling them in the electoral rolls of the concerned constituency. The act says the right to vote as demanded by the citizens of India living abroad is "their legitimate right." Conferring such right will enable them to participate in the democratic process of elections in their motherland and will also boost their involvement in the nation building.[43]

M. Right to reject or NOTA. (None of the above)

None of the above (NOTA) option was debuted in legislative assembly elections to Delhi, Rajasthan, Madhya Pradesh, Chhattisgarh and Mizoram.[44]

The Supreme Court held that the provisions of Rule 49-O under which an elector not wishing to vote for any candidate had to inform the Presiding Officer about his decision, are ultra vies Article 19 of the Constitution and Section 128 of the Representation of the People Act, 1951. As per the provisions of clause (a) of Rule 64 of Conduct of Elections Rules, 1961, read with Section 65 of the Representation of the People Act, 1951, the candidate who has polled the largest number of valid votes is to be declared elected by the Returning Officer. Therefore, even if the number of electors opting for NOTA option is more than the number of votes polled by any of the candidates, the candidate who secures the largest number of votes has to be declared elected. Under the provisions of Section 53(2) of RP Act, 51, if the number of contesting candidates is equal to the number of seats to be filled, the Returning Officer has to declare all the contesting candidates to be duly elected. In the case of elections to the Lok Sabha and Legislative Assemblies, in cases where there is only one contesting candidate in the fray, the Returning Officer has to, in accordance with the provisions of the said Section 53(2), declare the sole contesting candidates as elected. The provision of NOTA option which is an expression of decision not

---

[43]Times of India.NRI'S can now vote back home. PTi | Feb 4, 2011, 11.38 AM I ST 1 may 2014

< http://timesofindia.indiatimes.com/nri/us-canada-news/NRIs-can-now-vote-back-home/articleshow/7423807.cms>

[44] 25 april 2014 <http://www.erewise.com/current-affairs/elections-and-elector al-reforms-in- indiaart52c136657625a.html#.Uxy1T_mSzL4>

to vote for the contesting candidates is not relevant in such cases.[45]

4 PUBLIC VIEWS REGARDING ELECTORAL REFORMS

A. Public views regarding Electoral Reforms.

In order to get the views of general public over the electoral reforms in India, The following questionnaire was devised. This questionnaire containing 12 questions was given to 100 people and their responses were collected respectively

Date………..NAME ………………………………………………..……..
AGE…GENDER…QUALIFICATION………….

---

[45]The election commission of India, press note.5 may 2014 <file:///E:/ma%2
0pics/ELECTION%20COMMISSION%20OF%20INDIA%20nota.pdf
>

S .No.	Question	Yes	No	Can't say
1.	Voting should be compulsory?			
2.	To avoid voting should be a punishable offence?			
3	There should be an age limit for candidature?			
4.	There should be a direct election for President, PM. and CM?			
5.	There should be a post entry training programme for winning candidates?			
6.	NOTA should be counted?			
7.	A candidate should be barred for ever from contesting elections if lags by NOTA?			
8.	Voting age should be lowered down to 16?			
9.	Voting should be open for a week?			
10.	Voting should be done online?			
11.	No person should be allowed to contest election if having criminal charges?			
12.	Parties should not be allowed to conduct road rallies?			

Signature of respondent

*The above questionnaire is meant for research purpose as only to know the public opinion over my research program, "The *Electoral Reforms in India*". No part of the personal information of the respondents will be disclosed in public.

Sheikh Muzamil Mohd.

M.Phil Scholar.

D.A.V.V Indore.

Signature ....

After analysis of the responses collected from 100 people through the questionnaire method, the following facts were drawn, which are represented in the following table;

S .No.	Question	Yes	No	Can't say
1.	Voting should be compulsory?	96%	04%	00%
2.	To avoid voting should be a punishable offence?	46%	46%	08%
3	There should be an age limit for candidature?	86%	12%	02%
4.	There should be a direct election for President, PM. and CM?	76%	18%	06%
5.	There should be a post entry training programme for winning candidates?	86%	10%	04%
6.	NOTA should be counted?	64%	28%	08%
7.	A candidate should be barred for ever from contesting elections if lags by NOTA?	44%	42%	14%
8.	Voting age should be lowered down to 16?	16%	80%	04%
9.	Voting should be open for a week?	32%	58%	10%
10.	Voting should be done online?	74%	20%	06%
11.	No person should be allowed to contest election if having criminal charges?	84%	14%	02%
12.	Parties should not be allowed to conduct road rallies?	52%	36%	12%

B. Summary

From the above table it is observed that 96% agree that voting should be compulsory and 4% disagreed.

46% people agreed that to avoid voting should be a punishable offence, while 46 % disagreed and 4% people could not answer.

86% people agree that there should be an age limit for candidature, while 12% disagree. And 2% could not answer, clearly.

When asked whether there should be a direct election for President, PM. and CM. 76% agreed, while 18% disagreed and 6% were neutral.

86% people agreed that there should be a training program for the wining candidates, while 10% opposed it and 4% could not make choice.

When asked that whether NOTA. Should be counted or not, 64% agreed while 28% disagreed and 8 % were not sure about their answer.

44% agreed that candidate should be barred for ever from contesting elections if he lags by NOTA. While 42%, disagreed. And 14% could not answer.

Only 8% people were in favor of lowering down the voting age to 16, while majority of 80% were against and 4% could not make choice.

When asked whether voting should be open for a week, 16% people said yes, while 58% said no and 10% said that they cannot say anything.

A majority of 74% favored online voting proposal while 20% declined and 6% could not make any choice.

84% agreed that a person with criminal charges should not be allowed to contest elections, while 14% disagreed and only 2% could not make any choice.

52% people agreed that parties should not be allowed to conduct road rallies, while 36% disagreed and 12% kept silent.

5 SUGGESTIVE ELECTORAL REFORMS

Suggestive reforms

As per the public opinion and suggestive recommendations of election commission of India, the following electoral reforms can b introduced/should be introduced in the Indian electoral system? These suggestions should be taken into consideration for making electoral system free and fair manner:

These are;

At Present, the EC does not have independent staff of its own. Whenever elections take place, the Election Commission has to depend upon staff of Central and State Governments. The dual responsibility of the administrative staff, to the government for ordinary administration and to the EC for electoral administration is not conducive to the impartiality an efficiency of the Commission. Along with it comes the problem of disciplinary control over the staff deputed to do election work which generally generates confrontation between the Government and the BC. Now, when the elections have ceased to be a mere periodical affair, it is desirable .that the BC should have a permanent electoral administration with adequate disciplinary control over the staff.

☐ Efficient Electoral Commission is a requirement of the day to conduct free and fair elections. Democracy and fearless elections cannot exist without each other. To stop unfair practices in elections like rigging by using official machinery and to ensure existence of democracy, following methods or means should be adopted.

☐ The CEC should not be at the mercy to Executive and Parliament for its requirements. He should have separate and independent election department to enhance its objectivity and impartiality.

☐ Political corruption should be stopped by providing funds to genuine candidates through political parties whose account should be auditable. Candidate involving in corruption should be disqualified.

☐ for having a true democracy the registration and recognition of the political parties should be fair and without any kind of influence.

51

☐ Mass Media should play a non-partisan role in election and as a safeguard of democracy.

☐ Periodic elections are the foundation of a democratic system. For fair electoral system every aspiring candidate must have fettered freedom to offer himself as a candidate for election and to conduct his election campaign in his own way so long as he keeps him within the law.

☐ Every voter must be perfectly free to vote as Eve likes without any fear of consequences and without being unduly influenced by anyone by improper means and inducement or pressure of any kind.

☐ The secrecy of voters" preference to any candidate should be maintained. The election machinery must function honesty and impartially at every stage.

☐ Parliament must pass a law dealing with this serious problem of de-listing of valid electorates from electoral rolls because illiterate electorate residing in far villages cannot watch over publication of electorate lists.

☐ Preparation of electoral rolls by EC are to be supervised at village level and certificates from officials who prepare electoral rolls to the effect that the electoral rolls have been thoroughly revised. They do not include that persons and legally disenfranchised citizens and intentionally no name should be left in them. Accountability to be fixed for intentional exclusion of name of voters from electoral rolls.

☐ The names of the voters may be included in the electoral rolls even at the time of casting of votes by the polling officer, when he finds a genuine case.

☐ Unearth and confiscate black money, which is widely used for buying votes.

☐ Make politicians as well as voters, law abiding.

☐ strictly apply the Code of Conduct and punish those who violate it.

☐ Revise voters" lists in time to avoid bogus polling and correct mistakes in the lists.

☐ Prompt action by the judiciary if any kind of violation is detected during elections.

☐ Declare elections results in mandatory.

The following are the proposed electoral reforms by Election Commission of India;

1. Affidavits to be filed by candidates on criminal antecedents, assets, etc.

2. Need to increase the security deposit of candidates.

3. Criminalization of politics

4. Restriction on the number of seats from which one may contest.

5. Timely restriction on exit polls and opinion polls.

6. Prohibition of surrogate advertisements in print media.

7. Appointment of appellate authority in districts against orders of Electoral Registration Officers.

8. Compulsory maintenance of accounts by political parties and audit thereof by agencies specified by the election commission.

8. Government sponsored advertisements.

10. Political advertisements on television and cable network.

11. Composition of election commission, and constitutional protection of all members of the commission, and independent secretariat for the commission.
12. Expenses of election commission to be treated as charged.

13. Ban on transfers of election officers on the eve of elections.[46]

Following are the suggestive electoral reforms as drawn out of public opinion,

14. Voting should be compulsory.

15. To avoid voting should be a punishable offence.

16. There should be an age limit for candidature.

---

[46] Election commission of India. 25 june 2014 <http://eci.nic.in/eci_main/PRO POSED_ELECTORAL_REFORMS.pdf>

17. There should be a direct election for President, PM. and CM.

18. There should be a post entry training programme for winning candidates.

19. NOTA should be counted.

20. No person should be allowed to contest election if having criminal charges.

21. Parties should not be allowed to conduct road rallies.

22. Voting should be done online.

6 CONCLUSIONS

Conclusion

The electoral process in India is always being fascinating story, no matter whether it's national or state level. There is no other single event in India which offers such great excitements, interests and thrill. Elections have contributed a lot to national cohesion and growth of democratic temper.

Free and fare elections are integral part to democracy. It is through elections, a free modern state is created or at least hopes to create amongst its citizens a sense of involvement in public affairs. Again, it is through popular elections that an elected government is clothed with authority and legitimacy. Elections symbolize the renewal of the consent of people, the only basis on which rests the claim of the rulers to govern in modern times. Furthermore imparts continuity in governance for it ensures peaceful, orderly replacement of the government and makes possible a smooth transfer of authority to new set of new leaders.

It is beyond doubt that free and fare elections are the cornerstones of democratic polity. It is also perhaps the most effective and undoubtedly the ultimate method of controlling and regulating the conduct of political elites. It's true that once the mandate for political governance is given, the ruling elites have more or less free hand, subject, of-course, to the constraints of the Constitution and operates laws, to carry on the business of governance as they please.

The electoral system provides the mechanism which makes election possible. It specifies the officers/positions which are to b elected, the voters who are entitled to vote, the method as to how they would be vote, the constituencies from where the officials would be elected, the way the elections would be held. The electoral system, in fact includes both the election and electioneering. The elections make the representation possible.

Democracy advocates democratically elected governments which are responsible to elected parliament and state legislature. Free and fare elections are forming the bed rock for all democratically elected governing bodies. Therefore the, constitution of India has given due importance to this aspect of free and fare elections by developing a separate part (part xv) to elections. To carry out the constitutional mandate of free and fare elections, the constitution created an

55

independent constitutional authority, the election commission of India, to conduct elections to the offices of president vice president and to the parliament and state legislature.(realizing the importance of free and fare elections even to Panchayats and Municipalities, parliament amended the constitution in 1992 to create a similar independent constitutional authority, state election commission for each state to conduct elections to panchayats and municipalities.)

The conduct of elections in India after independence became the responsibility of the Election Commission. It was in 1950 that the Election Commission of India was set up as a constitutional body and entrusted with the task of superintendence, direction and control of all national and state level elections. It was also given the work of preparation and revision of electoral rolls. The Constitution has pro-vision for a single election commissioner to manage elections for both Parliament and the state legislatures. There was much discussion in the Constituent Assembly regarding the set-ting up of a single body to handle elections at both the levels. Some members of the Constituent Assembly saw this as a move towards an uncalled for centralization, but the proposal was carried forth. The election commissioner has "considerable autonomy of action" as it derives its authority directly from the Constitution.

The Election Commission consists of the Chief Election Commissioner and such number of Election Commissioners, if any, as the President may fix from time to time. The Chief Election Commissioner stands at the apex of the hierarchy of the Election Commission of India. All these commissioners are appointed by the President subject to the provisions of any law enacted by Parliament for the purpose. Indeed, the President appoints them at the behest of the Prime Minister because it is a constitutional necessity under the Parliamentary system of government which India has adopted. Chief Election Commissioner acts as the Chairman of the Election Commission in case any other Election Commissioner besides him is appointed.

In a democratic country like India, people have the real power and choice to elect their representatives. By this only the real welfare state will arise. Because now a-days people all over the world want welfare state only.

India is a vast country with a population of 1.22 billion as per 2011 census. It has 28 states and 7 union territories with 545 constituencies for elections to central legislature and more than 5200 constituencies to state legislatures. So far, elections to Lok Sabha (House of People) were held

15 times, the last being held in 2009. Even in the first elections of independent India (1951-52), there were 489 voting constituencies for Lok sabha and 5,283 constituencies of state legislatures. In the 1951-52 elections, there were 1,800 candidates contested for 489 seats of Lok Sabha and 15000 candidates for 5283 seats of states legislatures.

Till a few decades ago, India was considered to be a under developed country with a huge illiterates, rural oriented tradition-bound and Caste-ridden population. Vast distances involved the inaccessible terrain in several constituencies, problems of mobilizing sufficient staff for election duty and providing security—all these are major obstacles for conducting free and fair elections.

People observed serious malpractices in elections and there was criticism in the parliament and by the press and intelligentsia. However, the election commission gained a wide knowledge of difficulties of conducting elections year by year. After conducting several Lok Sabha and State Assembly elections, the election commission also realized the necessity of urgent reforms.

In order to make electoral system more transparent, the Government has appointed committees like Justice Tarkunde Committee (1975) and Dinesh Goswami Committee (1990) recommended extensive electoral reforms.

As per the public opinion, the following electoral reforms can be introduced/should be introduced in the Indian electoral system? These suggestions should be taken into consideration for making electoral system free and fair manner

➢ Voting should be compulsory.

➢ To avoid voting should be a punishable offence.

➢ There should be an age limit for candidature.

➢ There should be a direct election for President, PM. and CM.

➢ There should be a post entry training programme for winning candidates.

➢ NOTA should be counted.

➢ No person should be allowed to contest election if having criminal charges.

➢ Parties should not be allowed to conduct road rallies.

➢ Voting should be done online.

These reforms will considerably transform the electoral process in India towards the betterment, But India being a vast country with a multi-religious, multi-cultural, multi-lingual, multi-ethnic makeup, there is always a continuous need for newer and newer electoral reforms as to meet its dynamic nature and match the pace with modernizing time tide.

BIBLIOGRAPHY

1. Arora, N.D. Political Science. New Delhi: Tata Megraw Hill Education Private Ltd., 2012.
2. Bhagat, Anjana kaw. Elections and electoral reforms in India. New Delhi: Vikass publishing house pvt.ltd., 1996.
3. Bhagwati jagdesh N, Desai Padma & others.Electoral Politics in Indian states- Thre Disadvatagiuos Sectors. Luknow: Manohar book service,1975.
4. Bhalla, R.P. Elections In India (1950-1972). New Delhi: S.chand and co.Pvt.ltd., 1973.
5. Dikhshit, R.D. Geography of Elections - The Indian Context. Delhi: Rawat publications Jaipur, 1995.

6. Dr.Fadia, B.L. Indian Government And Politics.Agra: Sahitiya Bhawan, 2013.
7. Field John Osgood, Franda Marcus. F. Electoral Politics In Indian States- the communist parties of West Bengal. Delhi: Manohar Book Service, 1974.
8. Gehlot, N.S. Elections and Electoral Administration in India. New Delhi: Deep and Deep publications, 1992.
9. Giri V Shanker, Giri. V.V. The Voice OF Conscience. Madrass: Vyasa Publication, 1971.
10. Gupta, R.L. Politics Of Commitment(a study based on fifth general elections in India). New Delhi: Trimurti Publications, 1972.
11. Jennings M Kent, Herman. Ziegler. The Electoral Process. London: Printice hall INC. Eaglewood cliffs NJ, 1996.
12. Kashyap, Subhash C. Election and Electoral Refoms in India. Delhi: Sterlin Publishers private limited, 1971.
13. Masodkar, B.A. The Supreme Court On Election Law(as pronounced by the supreme court) 1952-1966. Indore: Law Book Sellers and Publishers, 1967.
14. Norman A, LLM. Solicitor. Parliamentary Elections. London: Shaw and Sons limited. 1995.
15. Palmer, Norman D. Elections And Political Development – The South Asian Experience. New Delhi Vikaas Publishing House, 1976.
16. Paul, Sharda. General Elections in India. New Delhi: Associate Publishing house, 1942.
17. Rajput, R.S. Dynamics of Politics in India-a study of 1984 and 1985 lok sabha elections. New Delhi: Deep and Deep publications, 1986.
18. Ross, J.F.S. Elections and Electors Studies in Democratic Representation. London: Eyre And Spottiswoode, 1995.

19. Roy, Meenu. Elections 1998 A coutinuety in Coliation. New Delhi: National Publishing Jaipur House, 1988.
20. Roy, Ramashrey. The Uncertain Verdict. New Delhi: Orient Longman ltd., 1972.
21. Sirsikar,V.M. Sovereignty without Crowns- A behavioural analysis of Indian electoral process. Bombay: Popular Prakashan, 1973.
22. Venkatarangaiya, M. Free and Fare Elections. Govt of India: Publication Division, ministry of information and broadcasting, 1996.
23. Verma S.P, Bhambri. C.P. Elections And Political Consciousness In India- A Study. Calcutta: Meenakhi Prakashan , 1967.

24. Wh Moris Jones, B.Gupta. India's Political Areas. Asian Survey: Interim Report on An Echological Investigation June , 1969.

ONLINE SOURCES

1. Election commission of India, http://eci.nic.in/eci_main/PROPOSED_ELECTORAL_REFORMS.pdf

2. Fadia, BL. Reforming Election Commission.<http://archive.indianexpress.com/news/antidefection-law/339606/>

3. Katju, manjari. Election Commission and Functioning of Democracy. < https://www.jstore.org/stable/4418140>

4. Rajgopal, Krishan Das. Anti defection Law.<http://archive.indianexpress.com/news/antidefection-law/339606/ >

5. Rao Pedamalla Sreenivasa, Mohammad. Masliuddin. Electoral Reforms and Legislative Resolutions in a Big DemocraticIndia: An Analysis. <file:///C:/Users/indore/Downloads/3334-5371-1-PB%20(1).pdf>

6. Singh, Bimal Prasad."Electoral Reforms in India – Issues and Challenges". International Journal of Humanities and Social Science Invention. ISSN (Online): 2319 – 7722, ISSN (Print): 2319 – 7714 <www.ijhssi.org >

7. The election commission of India, press note.<file:///E:/ma%20pics/ELECTION%20COMMISSION%20OF%20INDIA%20nota.pdf>

8. Times of India. NRI'S can now vote back home. PTI | Feb 4, 2011, 11.38 AM IST<http://timesofindia.indiatimes.com/nri/us-canada-news/NRIs-can-now-vote-back-home/articleshow/7423807.cms>

9. <http://en.wikipedia.org/wiki/Sixtyfirst_Amendment_of_the_Constituti
    on_of_India>

10. <http://pibmumbai.gov.in/English/PDF/E2014_FR17.PDF

11. <http://eci.nic.in/eci_main/eci_publications/books/miscell/elections-
    india.pdf>

12. <http://pibmumbai.gov.in/English/PDF/E2014_FR17.PDF>

13. <http://eci.nic.in/eci_main/eci_publications/books/miscell/elections-
    india.pdf>

14. <http://delhiassembly.nic.in/antidefection.htm>

15. <http://www.careerlauncher.com/lstcontent/plansuppliments/attachme
    nts/50/64/Anti-defection%20law.PDF>

16. <http://www.erewise.com/current-affairs/elections-and-electoral-
    reforms-in-india_art52c136657625a.html#.Uxy1T_mSzL4>

17. <http://www.wikipedia.org.in>

ABOUT THE AUTHOR

The author has recently completed his M.Phil from D.A.V.V University (Davi Ahilya Vishwavidyalaya) Indore-India. He is a Kashmiri citizen and belongs to a farmer's family living in a remote village situated in southern dist. Of Kashmir called Islamabad (Anantnag). He stated from a govt. school and had his graduation from Kashmir University. Besides his subject of study (political science) the author also writes Urdu and Kashmiri poetry.

www.ingramcontent.com/pod-product-compliance
Lightning Source LLC
Chambersburg PA
CBHW050516290526
45786CB00007B/2592